Giving Reasons

An Extremely Short Introduction
to Critical Thinking

Giving Reasons

An Extremely Short Introduction to Critical Thinking

By David R. Morrow

Hackett Publishing Company, Inc.
Indianapolis/Cambridge

21 20 19 18   2 3 4 5 6 7

For further information, please address
    Hackett Publishing Company, Inc.
    P.O. Box 44937
    Indianapolis, Indiana 46244-0937

    www.hackettpublishing.com

Cover design by Maura Gaughan
Interior design by Laura Clark
Composition by William Hartman

Library of Congress Cataloging-in-Publication Data

Names: Morrow, David R., author.
Title: Giving reasons : an extremely short introduction to critical
    thinking / by David R. Morrow.
Description: Indianapolis : Hackett Publishing Co., Inc., 2017.
Identifiers: LCCN 2017006933 | ISBN 9781624666223 (pbk.)
Subjects: LCSH: Critical thinking. | Reasoning. | Thought and
    thinking.
Classification: LCC B105.T54 M67 2017 | DDC 153.4/2—dc23
LC record available at https://lccn.loc.gov/2017006933

∞

Contents

Acknowledgments

Even a book as short as this one requires the efforts of many people. I'm grateful for the encouragement, support, and assistance of my editors at Hackett, Deborah Wilkes and Maura Gaughan. Thanks also to Jodie Allen for copyediting and to Laura Clark and Liz Wilson at Hackett for their hard work in making this book a reality. Many people, including Michael Reno, Nicole Aitken, Tyler Andrews, Maria Mikolchak, Heather Rainey, Susana Nuccetelli, John Strauch, Hans-Herbert Kögler, Anika Waltz-Cummings, Laura Novak, and John Mariana provided helpful comments on drafts of the book. I owe a great deal to James Freeman, Alan Hausman, Steve Cahn, and Anthony Weston, among many others, for teaching me to teach people how to think critically. Finally, I'm forever grateful to my parents, my students, and my children for teaching me, each in their own way, about giving and asking for reasons.

Preface for Instructors

You can use this little book in many different ways in many different courses, depending on your and your students' needs. Maybe you'll want to work through the book over several class sessions or several weeks at the beginning of the semester, using the exercises at the end of each chapter to help your students grasp the material. Or perhaps you'll want to use the book as a reference guide throughout the semester, referring students to particular parts as necessary. Or maybe your students can speed through the material in a class session or two as a crash course in critical thinking before moving on to the main topic of your course.

The first four chapters of the book introduce students to the basics of argumentation. Chapters 5 and 6, respectively, extend those lessons to cover normative arguments and offer advice for interpreting other people's arguments charitably. Appendix A provides a brief guide to some common argument forms in deductive logic, and Appendix B introduces some common fallacies in informal logic.

Your students will benefit most from this book if you pair the text with opportunities to apply its contents to the specific topic of your course. In particular, they'll benefit from seeing you analyze and evaluate arguments related to the topic of the course, including arguments straight out of course readings, and from analyzing and evaluating such arguments themselves. One way to do this is to adapt the exercises at the end of each chapter by assigning specific topics or arguments to discuss. Another option is to assign excerpts from readings that you'll cover later in the course and ask students to analyze and evaluate the arguments they find there.

For exercises, helpful resources, and printable PDFs of the appendices, please visit the companion website at http://hackettpublishing.com/giving_reasons_title_support.

Introduction

One of the central goals of a good education is to improve students' ability to think for themselves. And it's not just philosophy professors like me who see things this way. When I talk to other professors—whether they're economists in a business school, doctors or nurses in a medical school, mathematicians, biologists, or whatever—they all want their students to learn to think for themselves. I hear something similar from professionals in all kinds of organizations: they want to hire people who can think independently, evaluate information, and offer solutions to problems they've never seen before.

Educators usually call this **critical thinking**. That doesn't mean being critical in the sense of being mean-spirited. The "critical" means "exercising careful judgment." It comes from the ancient Greek word *krités*, which means "judge" or "umpire." Learning to think critically means learning to be an effective judge of what you should believe. Not only is this way of thinking valued by educators and employers alike, it also enriches your life in other ways, and so is worth learning for its own sake. Learning to think critically is a long journey—one that you'll travel for your entire life, because you can always get better at it. The goal of this book is to help you get off on the right foot.

1

Facts, Opinions, and Knowledge

In a television spoof of the old movie *12 Angry Men*, a town's mayor stands accused of murder. Eleven of the twelve jurors think he's obviously guilty, but one of them insists on reviewing the evidence anyway. The case against the mayor seems damning: The murder victim had written a blackmail letter threatening to reveal the mayor's involvement in a corruption scandal. Furthermore, the murder weapon was a knife that belonged to the mayor. Although the mayor testified that he was innocent, most of the jurors assume that he's lying. "He's a politician," explains one juror. "They're all liars!" The skeptical juror replies that they should "be sticking to the facts."[1]

Lawyers sometimes tell witnesses the same thing: stick to the facts. They'll advise witnesses not to give their "conclusions or opinions" about the case.[2] But what, exactly, does it mean to "stick to the facts"? What is the skeptical juror asking his fellow jurors to do? What is the lawyer

1. "12 and a Half Angry Men," *Family Guy*, March 24, 2013, FOX.
2. U.S. Attorney's Office, "Tips for Testifying," http://www.justice.gov/.

1

asking when she asks the witness to give "facts" rather than "opinions"?

Some people would say that a fact is something that's been proven, whereas an opinion is something that hasn't been proven. But if you think about it carefully, you'll see that this is a mistake.

There are, after all, lots of facts that haven't been proven. Imagine, for instance, that you sit down with a bowl of noodles. There's some fact of the matter about how many noodles are in your bowl, but neither you nor anyone else knows what it is. To take a more exotic example, there's a fact of the matter about whether aliens have watched the television broadcast of the 1936 Olympics—one of the first television broadcasts strong enough to reach outer space. But no human has proven the existence or nonexistence of those aliens, much less whether they've watched the broadcast. Thus, there are facts that no one has proven.

> **FACTS**
>
> The facts are out there with or without our knowledge of them. There are even facts that nobody knows.

Furthermore, there are some facts that can never be proven. There's a fact of the matter, for instance, about exactly how many days ago the first human crossed the Colorado River. It must have happened thousands of years ago, but we'll never know exactly when it happened. And most likely, the first person to cross the Colorado couldn't have known that he or she was the first. Thus, no one has *ever* known exactly when this happened, and no one ever will. But there's still a fact of the matter.

A **fact**, then, is just something that's true, whether anyone knows it's true or not. Or more precisely, a fact is what's expressed by a true statement. In other words, to say that something is a fact is to say something about the way the world is, not about what anyone knows or has proven to be true.

An **opinion**, on the other hand, is just a *belief* that someone has, regardless of whether that belief is true or false, proven or unproven. For instance, you believe that the Earth is round, whereas the ancient Egyptians believed that the Earth is flat. So, you have a different opinion about the shape of the Earth than the ancient Egyptians did. This isn't to say that your opinion is no better than the ancient Egyptians' was: your belief is true, and theirs wasn't. In addition to being true or false, beliefs can be **justified** or not. Roughly, that means that the person whose belief it is may or may not have *good reasons* for holding that belief. If he or she has good reasons, we say his or her belief is justified; if not, not. Often, people reserve the term **opinion** (or **mere opinion**) for beliefs that aren't justified—that is, beliefs for which the believer doesn't have good enough reasons. Thus, to say that someone's belief is "just an opinion" isn't to make a claim about the way the world is (or isn't); it's to make a claim about the quality of that person's reasons for holding that belief.

> **OPINIONS VERSUS KNOWLEDGE**
>
> An **opinion** is simply a belief: some are true, some are false.
>
> A belief that's both *true* and *justified* is **knowledge**.

When someone has a belief that's both true and justified, we usually don't call that belief an opinion; we usually call it **knowledge**. That is, we usually say that you know something if it's true and you have good reasons to believe it. Thus, to say that a belief amounts to knowledge is *both* to make a claim about the way the world is *and* to make a claim about the quality of the believer's reasons for holding that belief. For instance, suppose a rookie cop on the bomb squad believes he should cut the green wire to disarm a bomb in front of him. But if his partner found out that he had just flipped a coin to decide which wire to cut, she should say that he doesn't *know* which wire to cut—even if he's right about the green wire. He only counts as *knowing* which wire to cut if he has good reasons to choose the green wire over the others. Determining whether someone knows something, then, involves more than figuring out whether their belief is true. It involves figuring out whether they have good enough reasons for believing it.

This, it turns out, explains why lawyers object to witnesses giving their "opinions." In a criminal case, a court of law is supposed to stick to a very high standard for justifying beliefs: the prosecution must prove its case "beyond a reasonable doubt." In everyday life, we might be justified in believing that a politician is lying when he denies knowing about some scandal. As the skeptical juror points out in the example from earlier, though, things are different in the courtroom. The jurors aren't justified in believing that the mayor is lying simply because he's a politician. They might *believe* that he's lying, but that belief isn't justified by the available evidence; their belief is "just an opinion." In saying that they should "stick to the facts," the juror means to say that they should stick only to things that they *know* to be true.

Notice, however, that the skeptical juror's suggestion to "stick to the facts" is somewhat misleading. Thus, it would have been better for the skeptical juror to say, "Let's stick to what we really know." After all, a fact isn't the *same* as "something the jurors know." There are facts that the jurors don't know. In particular, there's a fact of the matter about whether the mayor killed the victim. Only the mayor knows that fact. And even if the mayor were to drop dead, leaving *nobody* who knows whether he committed the murder, there would *still* be a fact of the matter.

Facts are one kind of thing; knowledge and opinion are another.

What does all of this have to do with critical thinking? In much of your educational experience, you've probably been asked to focus on learning the "right" answer so that you can recognize it on a test or repeat it back when asked. In many college courses and in many jobs, however, simply knowing the right answer isn't enough; you need to know and be able to explain *why* it's the right answer. That is, you need to be able to *justify* your belief in a particular answer. Being able to explain why an answer is the right answer is a crucial part of critical thinking. You also need to be able to reflect critically on the beliefs you already have to figure out which ones are mistaken or unjustified. That's a crucial part of critical thinking, too.

The shift from giving answers to giving reasons makes many people uncomfortable at first, as does the need to reflect critically on your existing beliefs. It requires a different way of thinking about the things you're learning and the things you think you know. Perhaps you used to be able to do just fine by treating the things you're learning as isolated facts—little independent bits of knowledge that you can memorize from flash cards, without much concern for the connections between them or the way they relate to your existing beliefs. If you were asked to give reasons for something, some of your teachers might have described the task as "giving your opinion" about the matter. And when you were asked for your opinion, your teachers may have implied that there were no wrong answers. In more advanced courses and on the job, however, people will judge for themselves whether your reasons are good enough for your opinion to count as knowledge. It can come as a big shock to have other people suddenly judging how good your reasons are, instead of just accepting them as your opinion.

Learning to be a critical thinker can help ensure that your reasons are good enough. Thinking critically means learning to give good reasons for your beliefs and changing your beliefs when you have good reasons to change them. Before believing something, critical thinkers ask themselves whether they have good reasons to accept the belief. If so, they accept the belief; if not, they don't. And just as importantly, critical thinkers also subject their existing beliefs to the same scrutiny, asking themselves whether they have good reasons to go on believing the things that they already believe. Sometimes this leads critical thinkers to give up their beliefs or to change them. At other times, it prompts them to seek out and find good reasons for their beliefs. In that way, critical thinkers not only come to recognize what the facts are, but they transform their beliefs from mere opinions into knowledge. Once you can do that, the idea of other people judging your beliefs isn't as frightening.

Exercises

1. Write down three facts that only you know, using a complete sentence to state each fact (e.g., "I ate waffles for breakfast this morning."). Then, list three facts that no one knows. Since you don't know these facts, you'll need to describe them indirectly (e.g., by writing "exactly when Bill Clinton's cat Socks was born" or "whether there's life on any of Saturn's moons").

2. Describe a real, fictional, or imaginary situation in which someone has a true but unjustified belief. Explain how the person came to have that belief, why it's true, and why they're not justified in believing it. For instance, you might write something like this: "In the movie *So I Married an Axe Murderer*, Tony reads an article in the *Weekly World News* about a serial killer who marries men and then kills them on their honeymoon. Tony becomes convinced that his friend Charlie's new wife is the serial killer from

the article and that he's in danger of being murdered on his honeymoon. It turns out that Charlie *is* in danger of being murdered on his honeymoon. Tony isn't justified in believing this, however, because the *Weekly World News* generally publishes fake news and is therefore not a trustworthy source of information."[3] Or more simply, "A juror in a bank robbery trial believes the defendant is guilty because she thinks he looks like a bank robber. In fact, he is guilty. Her belief is true but unjustified, because thinking that he looks like a bank robber isn't sufficient to support her conclusion."

3. Watch or listen to a show, podcast, or video that discusses current events (e.g., a news broadcast, certain talk radio shows, podcasts about current events, etc.). Write down two statements from the show that you think were mere opinions and two statements that you think expressed genuine knowledge—that is, two statements that the speaker wasn't justified in making and two true statements that the speaker was justified in making. Explain, in writing, why you think the first two were mere opinions and the last two were genuine knowledge.

3. While you only need to provide footnotes for this exercise if your instructor says so, you should know that this example comes from Thomas Schlamme, *So I Married an Axe Murderer* (Culver City, CA: TriStar Pictures, 1993).

4.   Form a group with three or four of your classmates.
     Working individually, write down the most surprising
     fact that you *know* to be true. Have each member of
     the group share his or her surprising fact, along with
     a brief explanation of *how* he or she knows it to be
     true. As a group, discuss whether each member really
     knows that fact. Then, choose the most surprising
     known fact to share with the class and explain how
     someone in your group knows it to be true. As a class,
     make a list of the various ways in which people claim
     to know these surprising facts. Optionally, discuss as
     a class which of these surprising facts the class as a
     whole is best justified in believing.

2

Justification

Because there's no air on the Moon, there's no wind. Because there's no wind on the Moon, the footprints that Neil Armstrong left when he walked on the Moon are still there—unless, of course, the Moon landings were faked, as people like Bill Kaysing claim. According to Kaysing, NASA conspired with filmmakers to make it seem as if American astronauts had gone to the Moon. All six Moon landings, he claimed, were actually staged in the Nevada desert as part of an elaborate hoax.[4] Everyone is entitled to their opinion, of course—including Kaysing. But not everyone's opinion is true, and not everyone's opinion is justified. Either Neil Armstrong walked on the Moon or he didn't. I believe Kaysing is wrong; I believe that Neil Armstrong and the other Apollo astronauts really did walk on the Moon. But how can I *justify* that belief? In answering that specific question, we can learn a lot about how to justify beliefs in general.

Occasionally, we're justified in believing something because it's true by definition. Call this **justification by**

4. Bill Kaysing and Randy Reid, *We Never Went to the Moon* (Pomeroy, WA: Health Research, 1971).

definition. For instance, we're justified in believing that all triangles have three sides because the word "triangle" just *means* a shape with exactly three sides and three angles. The same goes for the belief that blue is a color or that extraterrestrials, if there are any, come from somewhere besides Earth. Outside of mathematics, though, there aren't many important beliefs that you can justify simply by pointing to a definition. In particular, it wouldn't be very convincing to say, "But of course the Moon landings weren't filmed in Nevada. A Moon landing, by definition, requires landing on the Moon!" If I said that, someone like Kaysing would just switch to a different term, like "alleged Moon landings." So I'll have to look elsewhere to justify my belief that Armstrong walked on the Moon.

Sometimes, we're justified in believing something because we've seen it to be true with our own eyes—or heard it, felt it, smelled it, or tasted it ourselves. Call this **justification by perception**, because it relies on our direct perception of the way things are. This is how we know all kinds of things—for instance, that there are people in the room with you right now, that it's snowing outside, that the toast in the toaster is burning, and so on. Could I use justification by perception to justify my belief about the Moon landings? Probably not. I certainly didn't *see* the Moon landings with my own eyes. If you or I went to the Moon today—or if we had a telescope many times more powerful than the most powerful telescope ever built—we could see Armstrong's footprints for ourselves, along with golf balls, electric cars, photographs, and other things the astronauts left there. Short of going to the Moon, though, I can't use direct perception of the Moon landings or Armstrong's footprints to justify my belief that people walked on the Moon. (Even if we did see those things on the Moon, would that *really* justify us in believing that astronauts landed there? Could there be other ways for that stuff to have ended up there?)

You might be thinking, "Couldn't we just watch the old television broadcasts of the Moon landings? Would *that* count as justification by perception?" Not quite. Perception is sometimes deceiving: Earth doesn't *look* like it's round—at least not from where I am—and it doesn't *feel* like it's racing around the Sun at about 67,000 miles per hour. But it is! In general, if you're going to rely on justification by perception, you need to be confident that your senses aren't deceiving or misleading you. When Kaysing insists that the Moon landings were faked, he's insisting that our senses are misleading us when we watch films of the landings. So I'll need to do more than point to the television broadcasts and say, "But it sure *looks* like people landed on the Moon!"

Perhaps I could rely on other people telling me about what *they* perceived. Call this **justification by testimony**, because it relies on other people testifying about what they've perceived, like a witness in a trial. For instance, if you're talking to a friend on the other side of the country, and the friend tells you that it's raining, you're typically justified in believing that it's raining wherever your friend is. Could I use justification by testimony to justify my belief about the Moon landing? Neil Armstrong died in 2012, but Buzz Aldrin, who walked on the Moon with

Armstrong, is still alive. I'm sure he would be happy to tell me about the time he and Armstrong walked on the Moon. (Would *you* ever get tired of telling that story?) The other surviving astronauts who walked on the Moon during later missions would surely tell me about their experiences, too.

Here we have a problem similar to our problem with justification by perception: to rely on justification by testimony, we have to be confident that the people giving the testimony are telling us the truth—and that they are right about what they perceived. That's often an easy requirement to satisfy, as when you're talking to your friend about the weather. When Kaysing claims that the Moon landings involve an elaborate conspiracy, though, he's claiming that the astronauts involved are lying to us. So I'll need to do more than just say, "But Buzz Aldrin *told us* that he walked on the Moon!"

Sometimes we learn things from people who know what they're talking about, even though they didn't perceive it themselves. Call this **justification by authority**, because it relies on someone who can speak with authority on a particular subject. (I don't mean that they're "authority figures" in the sense that school principals or deans or police officers are authority figures, but only that they are sufficiently knowledgeable about the subject that we can typically believe what they say about it.) In fact, *most* of our beliefs are probably justified in this way—including beliefs the original justification of which we no longer remember. How, for instance, did you learn that George Washington was the first president of the United States, that dynamite is explosive, or that Earth revolves around the Sun? Presumably, you were taught those things by someone whom you could trust to be correct about the topic.

The difference between justification by testimony and justification by authority is that someone can be an authority on something without having directly *perceived* that thing. For instance, your history teacher can be an authority on early American presidents without having actually seen any of those presidents. As with testimony, though, the important thing is to be confident that the authority on whom you're relying is knowledgeable and trustworthy about the particular issue at hand.

IS MY SOURCE AN AUTHORITY?

Sources of justification by authority must be

1. Well-informed about the particular topic

2. Impartial—that is, unbiased

In general, you want to look for two main things to ensure that you've found a knowledgeable, trustworthy source. You want to ensure, first, that the source is *well-informed about the particular topic you're thinking about.* Just because someone is an expert in one area doesn't mean that he or she is an expert in another area, so look for a specific reason to think that the person knows a lot about your particular topic. For instance, professional astronomers or aerospace engineers could probably tell you a lot about various aspects of the Apollo missions, but that doesn't necessarily make them experts on, say, philosophy or politics.

Second, you want to ensure that your source is *impartial* or *unbiased* in the sense that their primary motivation is to find and communicate the truth about the topic you're thinking about, as opposed to pushing a particular answer or agenda. The dean of a college is likely to be well-informed about how her college compares to others, but she has a strong motivation to emphasize her own college's strengths and downplay its weaknesses. Note that both of these qualities—being well-informed and unbiased—can be easy to fake on the internet, so take special care when using online sources—especially online sources with which you're not familiar.

In the Moon landing case, I might look for people who have detailed knowledge of the Apollo missions, either because they worked on those missions or because they have studied the issue extensively. Such people are likely to be well-informed about the Moon landings. (Whether such people are impartial might be more difficult to assess in this case. Can you figure out why?) While almost all such authorities will tell you that the Moon landings were real, a few people who studied the issue extensively, including Bill Kaysing, concluded that the landings were faked. Sometimes this happens when we're seeking justification by authority. What should we do when the experts disagree like this? One thing to do is try to determine whether there's a general consensus among the experts. This doesn't mean that every single expert agrees—only that a large majority of them do. Especially when we aren't qualified to decide for ourselves, we're often justified in relying on the consensus of experts. In this case, the consensus of experts is that the Moon landings were real; only a small group of those who have studied the issue believe they were faked. This consensus of experts provides fairly strong justification for my belief that Neil Armstrong walked on the Moon.

I can do even better, though. The most important way to justify a belief is by giving convincing *reasons* for it. Call this **justification by reasoning**. When we can't rely on definitions, perception, testimony, or a consensus of experts, we need to look at the reasons for and against a belief. Consider, for instance, some of the reasons that Kaysing gives for thinking that the Moon landings were faked: Kaysing points out that you can't see any stars in the photographs distributed by NASA. This, he claims, is a reason to think that the photographs weren't really taken on the Moon. Is this a *good* reason to think the landings were faked? It's not. As many others have pointed out, the bright sunlight on the surface of the Moon would have "washed out" the stars in the photographs. (Try taking a photograph at night under a bright streetlight. The light will prevent your camera from picking up the stars in the background.) Similar points undermine most of the other reasons that people like Kaysing give to justify their belief that the landings were faked. On the other hand, there's a compelling reason to think that Kaysing is wrong: Faking the Moon landings would have required a massive conspiracy involving thousands of people—not just the astronauts, but the NASA engineers who worked on the mission, the politicians and administrators who approved and ran it, the Hollywood filmmakers, and so on—all of whom would have to have kept quiet about it for decades. If you think, as I do, that it's extremely unlikely that so many people could keep so big a secret for so long, then you have a very good reason to think that the landings were real. These reasons, ultimately, are what justifies my belief that Neil Armstrong, Buzz Aldrin, and the other Apollo astronauts really did walk on the Moon.

To sum up, we've identified five ways to justify your beliefs: by definition, by perception, by testimony, by authority, and by reasoning. Learning to think critically requires learning to tell whether any of these methods justify a particular belief. Most importantly, it requires learning to use justification by reasoning—that is, learning to give and ask for reasons when appropriate and learning to tell good reasoning from bad reasoning.

FIVE WAYS TO JUSTIFY A BELIEF

1. Definition
2. Perception
3. Testimony
4. Authority
5. Reasoning

Exercises

1. Identify one belief of yours that you can justify by definition, one that you can justify by perception, one that you can justify by testimony, one that you can justify by appealing to authority, and one that you can justify by reasoning.

2. Write down a belief of yours that you think is justified by one of the five methods described in this chapter. Be sure to say which method you have used to justify that belief. Then, state which *other* methods you could *also* use to justify that belief, and explain how you'd go about justifying your belief using each of those methods.

3. Write down a belief that you can justify by appealing to authority. Then, find three *different* authorities to justify that belief, making sure that they are well-informed and impartial. These could be books, newspapers, reliable websites, teachers, or other sources. Be sure to state which sources you used and why you think they are well-informed, impartial sources of information about the topic of your belief.

4. Form a group with three to five of your classmates. Tell your group something that they'd be justified in believing based only on your testimony. Have everyone else in your group do the same thing, writing down what each group member says. Share your group's list with the class. When you hear other groups' lists, think about whether those claims are really justified by testimony, as opposed to definition, perception, authority, or reasoning.

3

Reasoning

In *Star Wars: The Force Awakens*, resistance fighter Poe Dameron tells the rebellious Stormtrooper Finn that they need to rescue his droid, BB-8, which Poe had left behind on the planet Jakku. The droid, Poe says, is "a BB unit . . . orange and white: one of a kind." A few scenes later, when Finn returns to Jakku and spots an orange-and-white robot, he puts two and two together to realize that this is the droid he's looking for.[5]

Finn's realization depends on a very short chain of reasoning, which we can reconstruct as follows: Poe's droid is the only BB-type robot that's orange and white. This droid in front of me is an orange-and-white BB-type robot. Therefore, this robot is Poe's droid.

A chain of reasoning is called an **argument**. (Note that this is a very different use of the word "argument" from its ordinary English usage, in which it means something like "a verbal fight." Verbal fights may or may not involve reasoning, but there doesn't have to be anything combative about an argument in the academic sense of the word.)

5. J. J. Abrams, *Star Wars: The Force Awakens* (Burbank, CA: Walt Disney Studios, 2015).

Every argument is made up of at least two **statements**—
that is, two sentences that could be true or false. Some of
the statements in an argument are meant to count as reasons to think that one of the other statements is true. The
statements that are meant to count as reasons are called
premises. The statement that they're reasons for is called
the **conclusion**.

Take another look at Finn's reasoning to see how these
different parts of the argument work. For clarity, let's
rewrite his argument as a numbered list of claims:

premises

(1) Poe's droid is the only orange-and-
     white BB-type robot.
(2) This droid is an orange-and-white
     BB-type robot.
Therefore (3) This robot is Poe's droid. ◄——— *conclusion*

The first two statements provide reasons to believe that
the last statement is true. So, these three statements make
up an argument. The last statement is the argument's conclusion, and the first two statements are its premises. We
use the word "Therefore" to show that statement (3) is
the conclusion.

One important skill in learning to use arguments is recognizing and analyzing other people's arguments. Analyzing an argument means taking it apart to see what the
premises are, what the conclusion is, and how the premises
are supposed to justify the conclusion. (Note that this is
different than figuring out whether the premises are true,
whether we're justified in believing them, and whether

they *really do* justify the conclusion. We'll talk about all of that in the next chapter.) Argument analysis is a skill that you'll develop with practice.

As you're learning to analyze arguments, there are two techniques you can use to help you. The first is looking for **indicator words**, which are particular words or phrases that writers use to introduce premises or conclusions. Some words, like "because" or "since," often signal that you're about to read or hear a premise. Other words, like "therefore" and "so," often signal that you're about to read or hear a conclusion. Take a look at these very short arguments, with the premises and conclusions marked:

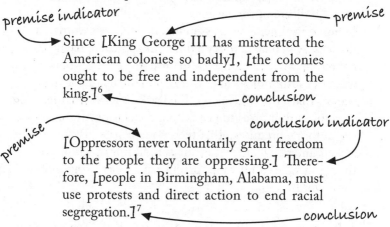

premise indicator — premise

Since [King George III has mistreated the American colonies so badly], [the colonies ought to be free and independent from the king.]⁶ — conclusion

conclusion indicator

premise

[Oppressors never voluntarily grant freedom to the people they are oppressing.] Therefore, [people in Birmingham, Alabama, must use protests and direct action to end racial segregation.]⁷ — conclusion

6. This is the basic argument given in the U.S. Declaration of Independence.

7. This argument is adapted from Martin Luther King, Jr., "Letter from a Birmingham Jail," April 16, 2013, https://kinginstitute.stanford.edu/king-papers/documents/letter-birmingham-jail.

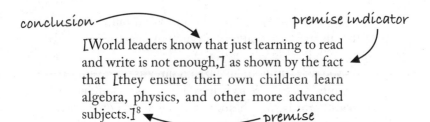

conclusion

premise indicator

[World leaders know that just learning to read and write is not enough,] as shown by the fact that [they ensure their own children learn algebra, physics, and other more advanced subjects.][8]

premise

The table on the next page lists some more indicator words.[9] Notice, though, that some of these words and phrases have other uses, too. Not every instance of "because" or "since" indicates a premise. Not every instance of "so" indicates a conclusion.

Some arguments won't contain any indicator words. In that case, you'll need to try a different approach: trying to figure out what the author's main point is. Ask yourself what the author or speaker is trying to justify or convince you of. That's the conclusion. Then, ask yourself what reasons the author gives to justify that conclusion. Those are the author's premises. This technique can be used with any argument, whether it includes indicator words or not, though it takes a bit more practice than just using indicator words.

8. This argument is adapted from Malala Yousafzai, "Nobel Lecture" (speech, Oslo, Norway, December 10, 2014), Nobelprize.org, https://www.nobelprize.org/nobel_prizes/peace/laureates/2014/yousafzai-lecture_en.html.

9. For an even more comprehensive list of indicator words, see Trudy Govier, *A Practical Study of Argument*, 7th edition (Boston: Wadsworth, 2013), 4.

PREMISE INDICATORS	CONCLUSION INDICATORS
because	therefore
since	so
for	thus
given that	hence
as shown by	consequently
due to the fact that	it follows that
may be inferred from	proves that
as indicated by	shows that
on the grounds that	we can conclude that
insofar as	we can infer that
assuming	which entails that
the reason is that	which means that

Most arguments are a bit more complicated than the ones we've considered so far. In particular, many of the arguments that you'll encounter have more than one step. For example, consider an argument that Hermione uses in *Harry Potter and the Prisoner of Azkaban*. While searching for an empty train compartment on the Hogwarts Express, which takes students to the Hogwarts School of Witchcraft and Wizardry, Hermione and her friends spot an unfamiliar man sleeping in one of the compartments. Ron wonders aloud who the man could be, but Hermione has already figured it out through a bit of reasoning: The man's luggage tag said "Professor Remus J. Lupin." So, he must be a professor. The students don't know him. So, he must be new to Hogwarts. And there was only one opening for new professors at Hogwarts that year—namely, for a new professor of Defense Against the Dark Arts. Therefore, Hermione concludes, the man must be the new professor of Defense Against the Dark Arts.[10]

You may have noticed that this account of Hermione's reasoning contains several conclusion indicators, each attached to a different statement. If we write her reasoning out as a numbered list of statements, it looks like this:

        (1) The passenger is on the train to Hogwarts.
        (2) The passenger's luggage tags say
            "Professor Remus J. Lupin."
Therefore (3) The passenger is a professor at Hogwarts.
        (4) Neither Hermione nor Harry nor Ron
            recognizes the passenger.
Therefore (5) The passenger is new to Hogwarts.
        (6) The only opening for a new professor at
            Hogwarts this year is for the professor of
            Defense Against the Dark Arts.
Therefore (7) The passenger is Hogwarts' new professor
            of Defense Against the Dark Arts.

---

10. J. K. Rowling, *Harry Potter and the Prisoner of Azkaban* (New York: Scholastic, 2001), 74ff.

In this more complicated argument, some of the statements are acting as both premises *and* conclusions. A statement that fulfills both of these roles in an argument is called a **subconclusion**. You can think of a subconclusion as the conclusion of a short argument that then gets used as a premise in another, longer argument. In Hermione's argument, statements (1) and (2) are premises for statement (3), making (3) the conclusion of a little argument. Statement (4) is a premise for statement (5), making (5) the conclusion of another little argument. Then statements (3), (5), and (6) are all premises for statement (7), which is the main conclusion of the larger argument. Don't be intimidated by these more complicated arguments. Just do your best to break them down into smaller pieces, and then try to fit those smaller pieces back together. It will take some practice, but you'll get the hang of it.

> ### SUBCONCLUSION
> A **subconclusion** is a statement within a multipart argument that acts as both a premise and a conclusion.

Not everything you read or hear will contain arguments. People do lots of other things with words. They describe the way the world is, they tell stories, they give commands, they make jokes, they give lists of facts, they make unsupported assertions about what's true, and so on. Another thing people do is give explanations, which are easily confused with arguments. Explanations aim to help someone understand *why* something is true, rather than helping them to see that it *is* true. (Confusingly, a set of statements can sometimes *both* explain why something is true *and* show that it's true, making it both an explanation and an argument.) To tell whether you're reading or hearing an argument, as opposed to a story, explanation, or something else, remember to ask yourself whether the author or speaker is giving *reasons* to justify some statement. If so, he or she is giving an argument.

Notice also that you can do lots of different things with arguments. The most common use of arguments is to try to convince someone else that something is true. When you use arguments in this way, though, you're not just asserting something or telling someone that they *ought* to believe it; you're giving *reasons* that should *convince* them to believe it. Another very common use of arguments is to arrive at a new belief by figuring things out for yourself. That's what Finn and Hermione do in the preceding examples, and it's something that you need to do a lot in college and beyond as you exercise independent thinking. Third, you can use arguments to examine your own beliefs, testing to see whether you really have good reasons to believe them. Fourth, you can use arguments just to see what follows from a particular belief. For instance, you can use arguments to see what *else* you'd have to believe if you accepted, say, Bill Kaysing's claim that the Moon landings were faked. This skill is crucial in academic and professional settings, too, as you encounter ideas that you want to understand, even if you don't necessarily believe them yourself.

This last way of using arguments—that is, to see what follows from a particular belief—is especially helpful in applying the abstract theories and general principles explored in many college courses. Suppose, for instance, you learn about the theory of libertarianism in a political philosophy class. Libertarianism is, very roughly, a theory that says that a government ought to act only to protect the liberty of its citizens, including the liberty to acquire and keep property. More specifically, this means that while governments should not restrict someone's liberty for their own good or take one citizen's property to promote another's well-being, governments may and should stop one citizen from harming someone else or stealing someone else's property. You can use arguments to figure out what libertarians would say about a particular issue, even if you personally don't agree with libertarianism. In thinking about

> Identifying premises as the foundations of arguments is important to analyzing given statements, but we can also treat general principles and abstract theories *as* premises for finding philosophical conclusions and real-life, practical solutions.

health care, for instance, you could reason as follows: *According to libertarianism, governments should not restrict someone's liberty for their own good. Even if forcing someone to pay for health insurance would benefit that person, forcing them to buy something they don't want is restricting their liberty. Therefore, libertarians would say that governments should not force anyone to buy health insurance.* The key here is to come up with a premise that connects some of the

basic ideas of the theory to the specific case you're thinking about (e.g., requiring people to buy health insurance
when they don't want to). This example illustrates how you
can use reasoning to understand the implications of different abstract theories that you encounter, which can
both help you draw conclusions about what you ought to
believe, reflect on your reasons for believing what you do,
and help you understand why other people believe what
they do.

To take another example, suppose that you're studying to become an elementary school math teacher and
that one of your textbooks encourages you to "present
rich, contextually authentic problem solving to students,"
meaning, roughly, that you should give your students
math problems that connect mathematical concepts to
things they have experienced for themselves.[11] This general principle becomes useful to you only once you can
apply it to particular cases. To do that, you can construct
arguments using the general principle as a premise. If you
were teaching in a big city where students rely on public
transportation, for instance, you might reason as follows:
*A good math problem will connect mathematical concepts to
my students' experiences. I want to teach my students about
the mathematical concept of averages. My students all have
experience with buses running late. So, I could create a good
math problem by creating a word problem requiring students
to figure out how late a particular bus is on average.* Again,

11. Kassia Omohundro Wedekind, *Math Exchanges: Guiding Young
Mathematicians in Small Group Meetings* (Portland, ME: Stenhouse
Publishers, 2011), 8.

the key is to come up with a premise that connects the general principle about presenting contextually authentic math problems to the specific case at hand. This simple example illustrates how you can use reasoning to turn the abstract, general principles that you learn in your classes into useful tools for solving actual problems in your life.

Exercises

1. Think of a movie that's playing this weekend that you think your instructor should go see. Write an argument the conclusion of which is that the instructor should go see that movie. (You don't have to think too hard about this! You do it all the time, when you're trying to decide what movie *you* should see or what movies to recommend to your friends or family.)

2. Chapters 1 and 2 of this book contain various arguments designed to convince you of different things. Find *one* of those arguments and rewrite it as a list of numbered statements, being sure to list the conclusion last.

3. Find a written argument on the internet. Good places to look include opinion columns on news sites, letters to the editor, blog posts, or social media. Print out the argument. Circle any indicator words. Bracket and label the premises and the conclusion, following the examples in this chapter. Then, rewrite

the argument as a numbered list of statements, being sure to list the conclusion last.

4. Form a group with three or four of your classmates. Have each member of the group write an argument in paragraph form, with or without indicator words. Pass your argument to the group member to your left; the person to your right will pass his or her argument to you. Then, *on a separate piece of paper*, rewrite your classmate's argument as a numbered list of statements, being sure to list the conclusion last. Pass your classmate's original argument to the left and take an argument from the person on your right. Rewrite *that* argument on your own paper. Repeat the process until you've analyzed everyone else's argument. Then, have everyone compare their numbered lists to see if they match each other and if they accurately reflect what the argument's original author meant to say.

4

Better and
Worse Reasoning

Before there was Sherlock Holmes, there was C. Auguste Dupin, an amateur detective who appeared in three short stories by Edgar Allan Poe. In each story, Dupin uses his reasoning skills to solve a crime that has stumped the police. In "The Purloined Letter," the police approach Dupin for help finding a stolen letter. The letter contains incriminating information, and the thief is using it to blackmail his victim. The police have reasoned as follows:

(1) The suspect will keep the letter near him.
(2) The suspect will want to prevent the police from finding the letter.
Therefore (3) The suspect will hide the letter in a secret location in his apartment.

On the basis of this reasoning, the police have ransacked the suspect's apartment but found nothing. When he hears this, Dupin cracks the case by reasoning as follows:

(1) The suspect will keep the letter near him.
(2) The suspect will want to prevent the police from finding the letter.
(3) The suspect knows that the police will scour every possible secret location in his apartment but will ignore anything in plain sight.
Therefore (4) The suspect will hide the letter in plain sight in his apartment.

On the basis of this reasoning, Dupin visits the suspect's apartment and finds the letter hiding in plain sight.[12]

Just as Dupin's better reasoning leads him to the letter, stronger arguments are more likely to lead us to the truth than weaker arguments are. That's why learning to distinguish stronger arguments from weaker ones is an essential skill in critical thinking. Expert critical thinkers know that a strong argument needs premises that are **reliable**, **relevant** to the argument's conclusion, and **strong enough** to support that conclusion.

A reliable premise is a premise that the argument's audience is justified in believing—that is, one that it's reasonable for the audience to believe. We can count a premise as reliable, then, if the hearer is justified in believing it

12. Edgar Allan Poe, "The Purloined Letter," in *The Gift: A Christmas, New Year, and Birthday Present* (Philadelphia: Carey and Hart, 1844), 41–61. Reprinted in Edgar Allan Poe, *Thirty-Two Stories*, edited by Stuart Levine and Susan F. Levine (Indianapolis: Hackett Publishing, 2000), 256–271.

according to one of the five ways we discussed in Chapter 2: by definition, by perception, by testimony, by authority, or by reasoning. We can also count a premise as reliable if it's common knowledge (e.g., that Shakespeare wrote *Romeo and Juliet* or that the Earth goes around the Sun). Conversely, we can count a premise as unreliable if any of those methods—that is, perception, testimony, reasoning, appeal to common knowledge, etc.—can easily show that the premise is false.

Note that reliability applies only to *premises*, not to conclusions or to arguments as a whole. The question of a premise's reliability is about whether that premise is a good starting point for an argument for a particular audience.

Reliability is a surprisingly tricky concept for two reasons. One reason is that a premise being reliable is slightly different than it being true. A premise can be true without the hearer having a good reason to believe it. For instance, it's true that exactly eight U.S. presidents have been born in Virginia, but most people don't have any good reason to believe that. You'd need to *give* them such a reason by, for example, showing them a trustworthy website that says how many presidents were born in each state. When it comes to reliability, then, the question isn't (just) whether the premise is true, but whether the argument's audience is justified in believing it.

> ## AUDIENCE
>
> Premise reliability is always about reliability *for a particular audience.* Unless the audience has a good enough reason to accept a premise, that premise is an unreliable premise for that audience.

To figure that out, focus not on whether the premise is true, but on how the argument's audience does or could *know* that it's true. Notice that a premise might be reliable for one audience but unreliable for another audience. For instance, it's common knowledge among atmospheric scientists that Earth's atmosphere is about 80 percent nitrogen, and so that statement would make a reliable premise for them; but it's definitely not common knowledge among, say, ten year olds. Unless you gave a ten-year-old child a good reason to believe that premise (e.g., by having a trusted teacher tell them that it's true), it wouldn't be a reliable premise for him or her. Thus, reliability is relative to a particular audience.

The second reason that reliability is a difficult concept is that even though reliability is relative to a particular audience, it's *not* subjective. That is, the same premise can be reliable for one person and unreliable for another person, but that's *not* because the first person believes it and the second person doesn't. People don't get to decide for themselves whether a premise is reliable for them. Instead, it depends on whether they're *actually* justified in believing it. By analogy, asking whether a premise is reliable for someone isn't like asking whether the person enjoys a certain food; it's more like asking whether the food is safe for the person to eat. Peanuts are safe for some people, but deadly for others, and that doesn't depend on what the person *thinks* about peanuts. Here's a concrete example of how this works: Suppose you buy a lottery ticket and walk home telling yourself that you have a good feeling about the ticket. Before officials announce the winning number, you aren't justified in believing that you have a winning ticket, no matter how confident you feel about the possibility; the statement that you have a winning ticket wouldn't count as a reliable premise for you. If, later on, you compare your ticket number to the winning number and discover that they match, *then* you'd be justified in believing that you have a winning ticket; the statement that you have a winning ticket would become a reliable premise for you. Until you show your ticket to the lottery officials, however, *they* wouldn't be justified in believing that you have a winning ticket; the statement that you have a winning ticket wouldn't (yet) count as a reliable premise for them. Thus, whether something counts as a reliable premise for someone depends *not* on whether that person thinks it's true, but on whether he or she is *actually* justified in believing it.

A premise is relevant to the conclusion when the premise provides *some* reason to think that the conclusion is true, either on its own or in combination with other premises.[13] A premise is irrelevant—that is, not relevant—if it provides no reason to think that the conclusion is true, even when combined with other premises. This distinction is easiest to see with some examples: Suppose you wanted to argue that LeBron James is the greatest basketball player of all time. The fact that he has won four NBA Most

---

13. Strictly speaking, this is a definition of *positive relevance*. A premise can be *negatively relevant* to a conclusion if it provides a reason to think that the conclusion is *not* true. But that's not the kind of relevance you want in an argument!

Valuable Player awards is relevant to the conclusion that he's the greatest basketball player of all time, since it takes a truly exceptional player to win four times.[14] The fact of his MVP awards by itself wouldn't be *enough* to show he's the best because a few other people have won four or more such awards and there are many other things to consider in deciding who is the best player, but it does provide *some* reason to think he's the best. The fact that James's foundation supports charities like the Boys & Girls Club, on the other hand, is irrelevant to whether he's the greatest basketball player of all time. It might be a reason to think he's a good *person*, but it doesn't make him a better (or worse) basketball player.

People sometimes confuse the idea of having a good reason to believe something with the idea of having a good reason to want something to be true. If, for instance, you promised your roommate that you'd wash all the dishes for a month if the Cleveland Cavaliers win the NBA championships next year, you have a good reason to *want it to be true* that the Cavaliers will lose. But that's not the same thing as having a good reason to *believe* that the Cavaliers will lose because your desire that the Cavaliers lose isn't relevant to the claim that they'll lose.

When you're trying to figure out how strong an argument is, you want to ignore all of the irrelevant premises. A strong argument gives you good reasons to believe its conclusion. Irrelevant premises give you no reason to

14. "Lebron Takes 2013 Kia Most Valuable Player Award," NBA. com, May 6, 2013, http://www.nba.com/2013/news/05/05/lebron -2013-mvp-award/index.html.

believe the argument's conclusion. So, they don't make the argument any stronger. You can just get rid of them.

Sometimes, however, you need to know a bit about the subject of an argument to tell whether a premise is relevant to the argument's conclusion. (This is one reason that it's important to get a well-rounded education. It makes it easier to evaluate arguments about all kinds of different things.) Consider, for instance, experts' doubts about North Korea's claim to have successfully tested a hydrogen bomb in January 2016. Governments around the world confirmed some kind of weapons test in North Korea, but experts argued that it couldn't have been a hydrogen bomb because the weapon exploded with the force of about 10,000 tons of dynamite.[15] In other words, part of the experts' argument went like this:

> (1) North Korea's weapon exploded with the force of about 10,000 tons of dynamite.
>
> Therefore (2) North Korea didn't successfully test a hydrogen bomb.

To understand why the premise is relevant to the conclusion, you'd need to know that most hydrogen bombs are far more powerful than 10,000 tons of dynamite. If you wanted to make this relevance more obvious, you could expand the argument as follows:

15. Akshat Rathi, "Why North Korea's Nuclear Test Probably Wasn't a Hydrogen Bomb," *Quartz*, January 6, 2016, http://qz.com/587398/.

(1) North Korea's weapon exploded with the force of about 10,000 tons of dynamite.

(2) Hydrogen bombs normally explode with the force of at least 30,000 tons of dynamite.

Therefore (3) North Korea didn't successfully test a hydrogen bomb.

Adding a premise like this is known as stating a **hidden premise**—that is, a premise that you must assume for the argument to be plausible, often because it's needed for some of the other premises to be relevant to the conclusion. Figuring out exactly what assumptions an argument depends on can take a bit of practice, but it's sometimes necessary to understand why the premises of an argument are relevant to its conclusion.[16]

Even an argument that has reliable, relevant premises can still be weak if those premises aren't strong enough to support its conclusion. This is the problem with the reasoning that the police used in "The Purloined Letter." Their premises were reliable and relevant, but they overlooked the possibility that the suspect would anticipate the police officers' own thinking and cleverly hide the letter from them by leaving it in plain sight. That's why premises given by the police didn't provide as strong a reason for their conclusion as they believed.

16. We'll return to the topic of hidden premises in Chapter 6. See pp. 57–59.

Unfortunately, it's impossible to say, in the abstract, what it takes for the premises to be strong enough to support the argument's conclusion. That's why it's better to think of this criterion as a challenge: How likely is it that the conclusion would be false, even if the premises are true? The less likely it is that the conclusion would be false, the stronger the argument is. (Logicians have a special name for arguments where it's *impossible* for the conclusion to be false if the premises are true. They call such arguments **valid arguments**. When an argument is valid and its premises are true, logicians call it a **sound argument**. Confusingly, some people use these words more loosely, calling premises "valid" or "sound" when they mean that they're reliable, or calling an argument "invalid" or "unsound" when they mean that it's weak. Studying formal logic can help you distinguish arguments that are valid in the technical sense from those that aren't.[17])

When it comes to specific arguments, though, you can approach this criterion by asking *what more you'd need* to know before you could reasonably accept the argument's conclusion. Often, as in "The Purloined Letter," this is a matter of identifying possibilities that have been overlooked. If there are relevant possibilities that you've

17. For some examples of valid and invalid arguments, see Appendix A. For more information, see Chapter VI of Anthony Weston, *A Rulebook for Arguments*, 4th ed. (Indianapolis: Hackett Publishing, 2008). For even more guidance and practice, see Chapter VI of David R. Morrow & Anthony Weston, *A Workbook for Arguments*, 2nd ed. (Indianapolis: Hackett Publishing, 2015).

overlooked or things that you still need to know, then the argument's premises aren't yet strong enough to support the conclusion. Consider, for instance, the argument that jurors in Manitowoc County, Wisconsin, heard in the 1985 trial of Steven Avery:

> (1) Someone attacked a local woman while she was out jogging in broad daylight.
> (2) The woman identified Steven Avery in a photo and in a lineup.

Therefore (3) Steven Avery attacked the woman.

As fans of the documentary *Making a Murderer* know, Avery turned out to be innocent. Years after his conviction, DNA evidence and the real attacker's confession led to Avery's release.[18] In hindsight, we know that the premises in the prosecutors' argument weren't strong enough to support its conclusion. What more might we have wanted to know at the time? Among many other things, we might have asked whether Avery had an alibi at the time of the attack, or how often people make mistakes in picking their attackers out of a lineup. Another way to put the same idea is to ask whether the jurors have overlooked the possibility that the woman who identified Avery had made a mistake. If the jury had asked themselves these questions or considered that possibility, they might have realized that the prosecution's argument wasn't strong enough.

18. "Eighteen Years Lost," *Making a Murderer*, December 18, 2015, Netflix.

It's easy to go overboard with this last criterion, though. In general, an argument's premises don't need to give us *absolute certainty* for us to say that they're strong enough to support the conclusion. This is why the philosopher J. L. Austin said that, when it comes to having a strong enough basis for a conclusion, "Enough is enough: it doesn't mean everything."[19] But just *how* confident we need to be varies from one context to another. In mathematics or formal logic, we do need certainty. Experimental physicists demand *near* certainty, but not absolute certainty. Judges instruct juries in criminal cases to accept the prosecution's argument only if it establishes the defendant's guilt "beyond a reasonable doubt." These are all very high standards. But if someone is trying to convince you that the bus will be here soon, or that *Pitch Perfect 2* is worth watching, or that the new Mexican restaurant in town makes good guacamole, you don't need that level of certainty. In general, you should demand stronger premises when the stakes are especially high or when it's feasible to provide (near) certainty. But when the stakes are low and (near) certainty is impossible, it's often reasonable to accept an argument

> **"ENOUGH IS ENOUGH"**
>
> How strong a reason the premises need to provide to satisfy the sufficiency criterion varies from context to context. Ask yourself how much proof you need *in this particular case* before it's appropriate for you to accept the conclusion.

19. J. L. Austin, "Other Minds," *Proceedings of the Aristotelian Society*, Supplementary Volume 20: 148–179.

that isn't quite as ironclad. In that context, one argument can be stronger (or weaker) than another because its premises are more (or less) reliable or collectively stronger (or weaker) than the other argument's premises.

To apply these criteria to a particular argument—including, perhaps, arguments of your own—you need to do three things: First, ensure that all of the premises are reliable. (Throw out the ones that aren't, though if the argument is about something important, you might want to spend some time seeing if you can *make* them reliable by finding more support for them.) Second, ensure that all of the premises are relevant to the conclusion. (Throw out the ones that aren't, but only after you've considered possible hidden premises that would make them relevant.) Third, ask yourself whether the reliable, relevant premises are collectively strong enough to support the conclusion. If so, the argument is cogent and you should accept its conclusion. If not, the argument is not cogent; it doesn't give you a compelling reason to accept its conclusion.

Exercises

1. Look back at the three short arguments given as examples in Chapter 3 (pp. 21–22). For each argument, write a short paragraph evaluating the argument—that is, saying whether the premises are reliable (for you), whether they're relevant to the conclusion, and whether they're collectively strong enough to support the conclusion.

2. Look back again at the three short arguments given as examples in Chapter 3. See if you can identify any important hidden premises in the arguments. If so, say what the hidden premises are and why they're needed to make the argument plausible.

3. Find a written argument on the internet. Good places to look include opinion columns on news sites, letters to the editor, blog posts, or social media. Print out the argument. Then, rewrite the argument as a numbered list of statements, being sure to list the conclusion last. Finally, write a short paragraph evaluating the argument—that is, saying whether the premises are reliable (for you), whether they're relevant to the conclusion, and whether they're collectively strong enough to support the conclusion.

4. Form a group with three or four of your classmates. Pick a subject that you think it would be a *bad* idea for you to major in at college. Using at least three premises, write the strongest argument you can for the claim that it would be a bad idea for you to major in that subject. Trade arguments with someone in your group. Write a paragraph evaluating the other person's argument—that is, saying whether the premises are reliable (for you), whether they're relevant to the conclusion, and whether they're collectively strong enough to support the conclusion. Finally, as a group, choose the strongest argument to share with the class.

5

Reasoning about Better and Worse

Once a year, thousands of people descend on New York City dressed as Santa Claus for a day-long pub crawl known as SantaCon. In 2013, the writer Jason Gilbert described SantaCon as "obnoxious," compared it to "spoiled eggnog," and suggested that New York City should consider banning the event. The next day, the *New York Times* published a page on the "Learning Network" section of its website encouraging students to distinguish between the "facts" and the "opinions" in Gilbert's article.[20] The authors of this web page don't say explicitly which of the statements in Gilbert's article are "facts" and which are "opinions," but they seem to have in mind a distinction that will be familiar to just about anyone who's been to high school: statements about how the world *is* or

---

20. Jonathan Olsen, Sarah Gross, and Katherine Schulten, "Skills Practice: Distinguishing Between Fact and Opinion," *New York Times*, December 13, 2013, http://learning.blogs.nytimes.com/2013/12/13/skills-practice-distinguishing-between-fact-and-opinion/.

was are said to be "facts," whereas statements about what is good or bad or about how the world *should* be or about who *should* do what are all said to be "opinions."

The distinction the *New York Times* was suggesting is between **descriptive statements** and **normative statements**. Descriptive statements are statements about the way things are, were, or would be under certain circumstances. Normative statements are statements about what is good or bad, about how things *should* be, or about who *should* do what.[21] In Gilbert's article, for instance, the statement that some 30,000 "Santas" participated in SantaCon in 2012 is a descriptive statement because it says something about how the world *was* in 2012. The statement that the city should consider banning SantaCon is a normative statement because it says something about what someone *should* do.

The table on the next page lists examples that might help clarify the difference between descriptive and normative statements.

Some of the descriptive statements in the table are true; they state facts about the world. Some of them aren't. Furthermore, it would be easy to justify a belief in some of the statements, but not in others. (Can you tell which is which?)

21. Some people reserve the term **normative statements** just for statements about how things should be or who should do what, using the term **evaluative statements** to describe statements about what is good or bad. We'll stick to the simpler distinction between descriptive statements and normative statements.

DESCRIPTIVE STATEMENTS	NORMATIVE STATEMENTS
In 2015, over three million children under the age of five died of easily preventable or treatable causes.	It's a bad thing when anyone—especially a child—dies of easily preventable or treatable causes.
Leonardo DiCaprio wrote the play *Romeo & Juliet* in 1595.	*Romeo & Juliet* is a better love story than *Twilight*.
German universities do not charge tuition, even to foreign students.	The American government should make college tuition-free.
There were approximately 700,000 abortions reported to the U.S. Centers for Disease Control and Prevention in 2012.	It's morally wrong to have an abortion.
Mafia boss Carlos Marcello hired Lee Harvey Oswald to assassinate President Kennedy.	Mafia boss Carlos Marcello was an evil man.
Unless humanity dramatically reduces its emissions of carbon dioxide in the next few decades, global sea levels will rise by about two or three feet by 2100.	Humanity should dramatically reduce its emissions of carbon dioxide within the next few decades.

What about the normative statements? Can they be true or false? Despite what some people think, that's actually a very difficult philosophical question, which we don't have space to address here. But notice that people can have better or worse *reasons* for believing a normative statement. We can even say that someone is justified (or not) in believing some normative statement, based on the strength of his or her reasons for believing it.

Consider, for instance, the scene in *Monty Python and the Holy Grail* in which King Arthur encounters Dennis and his mother in their "anarcho-syndicalist commune." Arthur argues as follows:

> (1) The Lady of the Lake gave the sword Excalibur to Arthur.
> (2) Whoever receives Excalibur from the Lady of the Lake has the right to be king and exercise authority over everyone in Britain.
> (3) Dennis lives in Britain.

Therefore (4) Dennis should do whatever Arthur tells him to do.

Premise (2) is the normative premise in this argument, because it's about who has the right to exercise authority over the Britons. Questions about who has what rights and who has what authority are normative questions because they're questions about what different people may do or ought to do. As Dennis points out, however, "strange women lying in ponds distributing swords is no basis for a system of government." Rather, the right to exercise authority over others "derives from a mandate from the masses"—that is, from the people being governed and not, as the second premise states, from the Lady of the Lake. Since Arthur has not received a mandate from the people of Britain, Dennis reasons, Arthur doesn't have any right-

EXAMINING NORMATIVE PREMISES

When evaluating arguments with normative premises, be sure to ask yourself whether you have good *reasons* to accept the normative premises. This is especially important when you're already inclined to accept the argument's conclusion, since that makes it tempting to be less critical of the premises.

ful authority over them and Dennis is under no obligation to do what Arthur tells him to do.[22] Here we have two people giving reasons for their different beliefs about whether Dennis should do what Arthur tells him to do, with one of them giving much stronger reasons than the other. (Can you explain *why* Dennis's reasons are stronger?)

Of course, just as Arthur and Dennis continue to disagree about Arthur's right to tell Dennis what to do, people disagree about many other normative statements. But notice that people also disagree (or used to disagree) about all kinds of descriptive statements, such as how old the universe is; whether the Earth goes around the Sun; how much, if at all, raising taxes on investment income would slow

22. Terry Gilliam and Terry Jones, *Monty Python and the Holy Grail* (London: EMI, 1975).

economic growth; whether there is a God; whether the Bible is literally true; whether people can be reincarnated; and so on. So the mere fact of disagreement doesn't show that it's pointless to discuss or think critically about normative statements.

In fact, we can give arguments for normative statements just as we do for any other kind of statement. Arguments for normative statements must meet all of the same criteria as arguments for descriptive statements: the premises must be reliable, relevant to the conclusion, and collectively strong enough to support that conclusion. But arguments for normative statements must also meet one more criterion: they must contain at least one normative premise. In other words, if you're going to argue for a conclusion about something being good or bad or right or wrong, you'll need at least one premise about what's good or bad or right or wrong. This is because you need a normative premise to connect the descriptive premises to the normative conclusion—that is, to show that the descriptive premises are relevant to the conclusion.[23]

Consider, for instance, an argument that Eazy-E gives in the film *Straight Outta Compton*. After New York–based Home Boys Only refuses to record Ice Cube's song "Boyz-n-the-Hood," Dr. Dre tells Eazy-E that he should record it himself. Eazy-E tries to convince Dre that this is a bad idea, arguing as follows:

---

23. The reverse is also true: if you're arguing for a descriptive statement, you need at least one descriptive premise. See the fallacy of wishful thinking in Appendix B.

(1) Eazy-E isn't a rapper.

Therefore (2) Eazy-E shouldn't be the one to record the
          song.

The conclusion of this argument is a normative statement.
It says something about what *should* or *shouldn't* happen.
The only premise is a descriptive statement. It says something about how the world *is*. But that descriptive statement is only relevant to the normative conclusion if you
think that the song should be recorded by a rapper. In
other words, to make that descriptive premise relevant to
the normative conclusion, we need to expand the argument to include a normative premise, as follows:

(1) Eazy-E isn't a rapper.
(2) The song should only be recorded by a
    rapper.

Therefore (3) Eazy-E shouldn't be the one to record the
          song.

It's important to recognize this hidden normative premise because it might not be correct.[24] In the film, Dre
responds to Eazy-E's argument by convincing him that it
would be okay for someone who isn't a rapper to record
the song—that is, that premise (2) is incorrect.[25]

---

24. For more on hidden premises, see pp. 57–59.

25. F. Gary Gray, *Straight Outta Compton* (Universal City, CA: Universal Pictures, 2015).

The main lessons from these reflections, then, are that normative statements (i.e., statements about what's good or bad or right or wrong or about how things should be) aren't necessarily mere opinions; that we can and should use reasoning to decide which normative statements to believe, just as we do with descriptive statements; and that when you're giving an argument for (or against) a normative statement, you'll need at least one normative statement in your premises.

Exercises

1. Pick two normative statements—one that you agree with and one that you disagree with. Write down a short argument for the first statement, putting a star next to any normative statements in your premises. Then, write down a short argument against the second statement, putting a star next to any normative statements in your premises.

2. Pick a normative statement that some people accept and some people reject. Write down one *strong* argument for that statement and one *weak but popular* argument for that statement, putting a star next to any normative statements in the premises of each argument. Then, write a short paragraph explaining why you think the first argument is stronger than the second argument.

3. In a newspaper or on a website, find an editorial or op-ed that argues for a normative statement. Print out or cut out the editorial or op-ed. Circle the argument's conclusion. Underline each of the premises in the argument, putting a star next to each of the normative premises. Then, write a short paragraph evaluating the argument (i.e., stating whether you think it's cogent or not and giving your reasons for thinking so).

4. Form a group with three or four of your classmates. Make a list of at least seven normative statements about which you all agree. Then, make a list of at least three normative statements about which you don't all agree. For each statement about which you do *not* all agree, have each person give one reason for accepting (or not accepting) the statement. Be prepared to share your lists and your reasons with your class.

6

Asking for Reasons

After escaping from an invading army, losing an eye and an ear to syphilis, and narrowly surviving a devastating earthquake, the fictional philosopher Dr. Pangloss assured his friend Candide that all of these disasters were "for the best."[26] Pangloss had often explained to Candide that theirs was "the best of all possible worlds," and therefore everything that happened must be for the best. But since he saw his share of sin and suffering in the world around him, Candide "often had occasion to notice that things went pretty badly."[27]

The French philosopher Voltaire published the story of Candide in 1759 to make fun of the German philosopher Gottfried Leibniz, who had famously said that our world was, despite appearances, the best possible world. In suggesting that Leibniz thought things never went badly, however, Voltaire misrepresented what Leibniz meant. Leibniz was trying to answer a serious question that has troubled many religious people: if God is all-knowing, all-powerful, and perfectly good, why is the world so full

26. Voltaire, *Candide* (New York: W. W. Norton, 2016 [1759]), 9–13.
27. Voltaire, *Candide*, 39.

of pain and suffering? His answer was, very roughly, that because all the events in the world are interconnected, it simply wasn't possible for God to create a world that was any better than this one. For instance, if God had created a world in which some particular bad event hadn't happened, God would have had to change some good things, as well, resulting in a world that wasn't as good as ours.[28] So, rather than saying that bad things never happen, Leibniz was saying that this is the best of all possible worlds *even though* bad things happen in it.

Voltaire himself may well have understood what Leibniz was saying, but the way he portrayed Leibniz's ideas in *Candide* was misleading. In misrepresenting those ideas, he does a disservice to anyone who is really interested in the question that Leibniz was trying to answer—the question of how God could allow evil. After all, if you want to find the best answer to a question, you need to find the best reasons for each possible answer. And if you want to find the best reasons for each possible answer, you need to interpret people's ideas and arguments in the way that makes them as powerful as possible. You need, in other words, the best of all possible interpretations.

Putting this advice to use amounts to applying what logicians call the **principle of charity**. The principle of charity says, roughly, that you should interpret someone else's arguments and statements in whatever way makes them strongest or most reasonable. That is, when someone makes an argument that could be interpreted in more

28. G. W. Leibniz, *Theodicy*, trans. E. M. Huggard (New Haven, CT: Yale University Press, 1952 [1710]), 128–129.

than one way, you should interpret it in a way that makes it as strong as possible; and when someone makes a statement that could be interpreted in more than one way, you should interpret it in the way that makes it most reasonable or most likely to be true. An interpretation that makes an argument or statement seem as strong or reasonable as possible is called a **charitable interpretation**; one that makes it seem particularly weak or unreasonable is called an **uncharitable interpretation**. For instance, the claim that nothing bad ever happens is obviously false; it was uncharitable for Voltaire to suggest that Leibniz held that view. The claim that bad things are necessary for other good things to happen is at least somewhat more plausible; to interpret Leibniz as saying that all bad things are counterbalanced by good things makes him seem at least a little more reasonable. So, according to the principle of charity, that's how Voltaire should have interpreted Leibniz.[29]

The principle of charity has a number of more specific implications. Adopting the following three practices will help you apply the principle of charity not only in conversations or classroom discussions, but also in one-sided

---

29. It's possible, however, that this is an uncharitable interpretation of Voltaire! Arguably, Voltaire understands Leibniz's real claim about good things counterbalancing bad things but uses the story of Candide to suggest that this claim is implausible. That is, perhaps Voltaire does understand Leibniz correctly and is indirectly arguing that many of the bad events in the world aren't really necessary, as Leibniz claims they are. As this example shows, applying the principle of charity isn't always easy, but it *is* always important.

forms of communication, such as when you're reading or watching someone's arguments.

First, when someone makes a statement that you think is doubtful, false, or even outrageous, confirm that you've understood the statement correctly and then try to figure out what reasons someone might have for believing it. For instance, the ancient Chinese philosopher Mencius famously claimed that humans are naturally good. Given the long list of horrible things that humans do on a regular basis, Mencius's claim might strike you as doubtful—it certainly seemed false to many of his contemporaries in ancient China. But if you read a bit about Mencius's ideas, you'll see that he meant this claim in a very specific way—a way that makes it much more plausible. Mencius meant that humans are born with the capacity to have certain feelings, such as compassion, that lead them to do good things and avoid bad things, and that someone who properly cultivates those feelings will develop into a good person.[30] If you had asked Mencius for reasons to believe this, he'd have pointed you to instances in which people spontaneously felt compassion (for example) and argue that these feelings are the "sprouts" from which good people developed their good character.[31]

Of course, *we* can't ask Mencius anything because he's been dead for over two thousand years. And even when you encounter claims or arguments by people who are still

30. Mencius, *Mengzi: With Selections from Traditional Commentaries*, trans. Bryan W. Van Norden (Indianapolis, IN: Hackett Publishing, 2008), 149.

31. See, e.g., Mencius, *Mengzi*, 7–15, 45–47.

living, you might not be able to communicate with them directly. If you could communicate with them, you could simply ask, "Do you mean . . . ?" and "Can you give me some reasons to believe that?" When you can't communicate with them, the best you can do is read (and reread) what they wrote, talk to other people about those ideas, and so on. In doing so, you might come to understand their ideas and arguments more clearly. Failing that, you can sometimes come up with a more reasonable version of what they said on your own and work out a decent argument for *that* statement.

After confirming that you've understood the statement and looking for possible reasons someone might have for believing it, the second practice implied by the principle of charity involves looking for hidden premises whenever you encounter an argument that seems too weak to support its conclusion. We touched on the topic of hidden premises earlier in the book, where we said that a hidden premise is, roughly, a premise that isn't explicitly stated but that must be assumed to make the argument plausible. As with finding the strongest

THREE PRACTICES IN CHARITABLE INTERPRETATION

1. Confirm you've understood the statement and try to find possible reasons one might have for believing it.

2. Look for hidden premises if the argument seems too weak to support its conclusion.

3. When you find a fallacy, take a closer look to see if you can find a good argument behind the mistake.

interpretation of a claim, finding hidden premises is sometimes (but not always) easier if you can communicate with whoever is giving the argument. In that case, you can explain that you think you're missing some of the assumptions behind the argument and would like to know more; or, if you think you can guess what the hidden premises are, you can simply ask whether the arguer is assuming this or that premise. If you can't communicate with the person giving the argument, then finding hidden premises is a bit more difficult. Ideally, you want to find a premise that's highly reliable *and* makes the argument as strong as possible. If you can't do that, then you want to strike a balance between the reliability of the hidden premise(s) and the overall strength of the argument.

An example will clarify this. Suppose that you read the following argument in a letter to the editor of your school newspaper:

> (1) A college degree is practically a necessity now.
>
> Therefore (2) College should be free for everyone.

As it is, this argument doesn't seem particularly strong. As charitable readers, we should now ask: What extra premise might we add to strengthen the argument? Consider three possibilities:

> (A) Anything that's a necessity should be free for everyone.
> (B) Many students must take on large amounts of student debt to pay for college.

    (C) The government should ensure that
        everyone has what they need to get a good
        start in life.

If premise (A) were reliable, then adding it to the argument would make the argument about as strong as you could want. But (A) isn't reliable, since there are many necessities that we expect most people to pay for. (Everyone needs somewhere to live, but that doesn't necessarily mean that *everyone* should get a place to live for free.) Premise (B), on the other hand, is reliable; it's common knowledge. But (1) and (B) together aren't strong enough to support the conclusion. So, adding (B) to the argument wouldn't give us a particularly strong argument. Premise (C) strikes a better balance between the reliability of the premise and the strength of the argument: Although it's not *obviously* true and many people would dispute it, one could make a strong case that something like this follows from the idea that the government should ensure equality of opportunity. Furthermore, since it connects premise (1) fairly directly to the conclusion, it strengthens the argument significantly. Thus, of these three options, the principle of charity says that you ought to take the letter writer to be assuming something like premise (C).

    The third practice implied by the principle of charity concerns how you respond when someone commits a **fallacy**, which is, roughly, a mistake in reasoning. (More precisely, each fallacy is a *pattern* of reasoning that involves a particular kind of mistake. A person commits a fallacy when he or she says or writes something that fits such a pattern, and an argument that fits such a pattern is said to be **fallacious**.) Many fallacies are so tempting or so common that logicians have given them special names.[32] For instance, people so often jump from a handful of vivid examples to a sweeping generalization that logicians have a name for arguments that fit this pattern: hasty generalization. Many stereotypes result from hasty generalizations; people notice that a few people from a certain group exhibit a certain feature (often because we've been told to look for that feature), and then they wrongly infer that all members of that group have that feature.

To take another example, people often respond to an argument by criticizing the person making the argument rather than the argument itself; logicians call such a response an *ad hominem* argument. (*Ad hominem* is Latin for "against the person.") Even if the criticism of the person is warranted, however, someone's personal flaws are rarely relevant to the strength of their arguments; if something is wrong with the argument itself, we should be able to point that out without attacking the person who gave it. As yet another example, logicians have a name for arguments that illegitimately infer that one thing caused another simply because the second thing came after the first thing: the *post hoc* fallacy, from the Latin phrase *post hoc ergo propter hoc*, which means "after this therefore because of this." Many superstitions probably resulted from this kind of reasoning; the old belief that malaria was caused by "bad air" (*mal aria* in an old Italian dialect), for example, probably arose because doctors noticed that

32. See Appendix B for a list of some prominent fallacies.

patients developed malaria after spending time in swamps and wrongly inferred that the noxious air of the swamps caused malaria. (In fact, people developed malaria after spending time in swamps because that's where the mosquitoes that spread malaria lived.)

When you notice that someone has committed a fallacy, it's tempting to immediately dismiss what he or she is saying. The principle of charity, however, requires you to take a closer look to see if you can find a good argument behind the mistake. In some cases, an argument might appear fallacious simply because it fails to include premises that it should. In other words, sometimes an argument appears fallacious because there are important hidden premises. For instance, someone commits the slippery slope fallacy when he or she illegitimately argues against performing some action, even though the action isn't bad in itself, because the action would inevitably lead to something else that's bad in itself. The difference between a slippery slope *fallacy* and a *legitimate* slippery slope argument is usually whether there's good reason to believe that taking that first step really will lead to a bad outcome. So, if someone gives a slippery slope argument that seems like a slippery slope fallacy, the first thing to do is always ask whether there's a hidden premise that would support the claim that doing one thing really will lead to a bad outcome.

In a second kind of case, an argument is fallacious because it includes premises that it *shouldn't*. For instance, the problem with *ad hominem* arguments is they involve irrelevant premises. Specifically, they reason from a statement that someone has some personal flaw to the conclusion that the person's *argument* is a bad argument. But a statement about the arguer's personal qualities is irrelevant to the quality of his or her arguments. So, we should simply throw out the premises about the arguer's personal qualities, as we do with all irrelevant premises. But it's possible that the response to the person's argument *also* included some relevant premises—that is, premises that criticized the argument itself. Once we've set aside the personal attacks, we can evaluate the criticism based on those premises alone.

In a third kind of case, a fallacious argument is simply a misguided way to express a legitimate argument. For instance, during presidential elections, people sometimes attack candidates' ideas by calling the candidates themselves "out of touch" and "elitist." On the face of it, this looks like an *ad hominem* attack. But if we interpret those complaints charitably, we might instead see them as an indirect way of saying that the candidates' ideas won't work because the candidates don't really understand the problems facing the average person. That, at least, is enough of a starting point to begin a real conversation about the reasons for and against the candidates' ideas. Thus, reinterpreting the argument is much more productive than simply dismissing it as a fallacy, which tends to end a conversation (and on a bad note!) rather than move it forward.

This isn't to say that *every* fallacy hides some kernel of truth. Some are simply bad arguments. But with a bit of charity, even fallacies can lead you to find good reasons.

That, after all, is the point of the principle of charity: to help you find the best reasons that you can.

Exercises

1. The ancient Greek philosopher Epicurus famously believed that the most ethical way to live is by pursuing pleasure for yourself. Write down the *least* charitable way you can think of to interpret that statement. Then write down the *most* charitable way you can think of to interpret that statement. Finally, write a short paragraph explaining *why* the first interpretation is uncharitable and the second one is charitable.

2. Find an example of an argument that leaves important premises unstated. You might find examples in your own conversations, in newspapers, in things you read or watch online or on television, etc. Write down the argument as it was originally given. Then, write down three possible hidden premises that the argument's author might be assuming. State which premise gives the most charitable interpretation of the argument and explain why.

3. Using the social media platform of your choice or a site that collects memes, find an argument that strikes you as obviously mistaken. Write down the argument as it was originally expressed. If you think the argument commits a specific fallacy, give the

name of the fallacy. Then, rewrite the argument in the most charitable way you can.

4. Form a group with three or four of your classmates. As a group, produce a list of five common political beliefs that strike at least one member of your group as ridiculous. Then, as a group, try to come up with the most charitable interpretation you can for each of those beliefs, along with the strongest argument that you can for each of them.

7

Conclusion

Much of the work that you do in college and beyond involves reading and writing arguments. This book has given you the basic tools to begin doing that work.

Many required course readings in college contain arguments, and that might be a significant change from the reading that you did elsewhere. Many introductory textbooks make claims without offering much of an argument for them, and you're simply expected to accept those claims on the authority of the textbooks' authors. More advanced courses, however, will present to you a variety of claims that need to be justified *and* different arguments used to justify them. You're *not* always expected to accept those claims or those arguments. Furthermore, in many college classes, your instructors will assign readings whose arguments and conclusions they don't accept themselves, precisely because they want you to study and evaluate the authors' arguments and conclusions.

Even in classes and in employment training exercises that seem like they're just about memorizing facts, it's important to think about the arguments for those facts and the assumptions within those arguments. Sometimes, you'll be given the arguments, and sometimes you'll have to figure out the arguments or look them up on your own. Even if you accept those facts on the authority of the textbook author or a new job supervisor, understanding the justification for those facts can help you understand them better and apply them more intelligently. To be a critical thinker, it's no longer enough just to know *what* is true; you'll need to know *why* something is true and *how* you know it.

Much of the writing that you do in college and beyond will involve giving arguments. By introducing you to the key concepts and skills in recognizing good arguments, this book has also given you the basic tools to begin constructing arguments of your own. When you do so, make sure that you're clear about exactly what the premises and conclusion of your argument are, and make sure that your arguments satisfy the conditions needed for a strong argument: they should have reliable, relevant premises that are strong enough to support your conclusion.

In addition to evaluating and making arguments, reasoning can also help you apply what you learn to new topics. The ability to apply existing knowledge and reasoning habits to new topics and disciplines isn't only a crucial skill in college, but in your personal, professional, and civic life as well. Throughout your educational and professional career, you'll probably spend a good deal of time learning about various principles and theories in economics, medicine, sociology, chemistry, philosophy, or whatever else you study or do. If you treat those principles and theories as premises, you can use arguments to apply those principles and theories to new cases. Once you can do that, you can begin to do more than simply repeat what your teachers have taught you. You can begin to figure things out for yourself as an independent, critical thinker.

Many skills take only a short time to learn but a lifetime to master. Reasoning is no different. And as with those other skills, learning to reason well requires one thing: practice, practice, practice!

Suggestions for Further Reading

If you want to learn more about reasoning, consider the following books.

Govier, Trudy. *A Practical Study of Argument*, 7th Edition. Boston: Wadsworth, 2013.

> Govier's textbook delves much more deeply into the theory of informal logic than any of the other books on this list.

Morrow, David R. *Moral Reasoning*. New York: Oxford University Press, 2018.

> This textbook provides conceptual and theoretical tools to help you reason more effectively about ethical issues.

Morrow, David R., and Anthony Weston. *A Workbook for Arguments: A Complete Course in Critical Thinking*, 2nd edition. Indianapolis: Hackett Publishing, 2015.

> Building on Weston's earlier work, this complete critical-thinking textbook contains the complete text of the *Rulebook for Arguments*, plus tips on applying Weston's rules and hundreds of exercises based on "real-life" arguments found in newspapers, films, etc.

Pullman, George. *A Rulebook for Decision Making*. Indianapolis: Hackett Publishing, 2015.

> Pullman provides flexible guidelines for reasoning about what to do, drawing on important insights into how humans actually make decisions.

Tindale, Christopher W. *Fallacies and Argument Appraisal*. New York: Cambridge University Press, 2007.

> Tindale explores a wide range of fallacies in great detail, going beyond the coverage provided in Weston's or Govier's books.

Weston, Anthony. *A Rulebook for Arguments*, 5th edition. Indianapolis: Hackett Publishing, 2018.

> Weston's classic book offers a quick, accessible introduction to good reasoning, with helpful guidelines for making arguments of various kinds.

If you want to investigate particular topics in more depth, ask your instructor or your librarian for further recommendations.

Appendix A

Selected Patterns of Reasoning in Deductive Logic

Deductive logic is the study of arguments that aim to establish their conclusions with complete certainty. To do this, they rely on certain patterns of reasoning that link the premises and conclusions together so tightly that the truth of the premises would *guarantee* the truth of the conclusion. We examine some of these patterns here.

MODUS PONENS	
(1) If **this** is true, then **that** is true.	(1) If <u>I am thinking</u>, then <u>I exist</u>.
(2) **This** is true.	(2) <u>I am thinking</u>.
Therefore (3) **that** is true.	Therefore (3) <u>I exist</u>.

René Descartes, *Discourse on Method and Meditations on First Philosophy*, translated by Donald A. Cress (Indianapolis: Hackett Publishing, 1999 [1637]).

MODUS TOLLENS

(1) If **this** is true, then **that** is true.	(1) If there are intelligent aliens in our galaxy, then we would have been visited by aliens by now.
(2) **That** is not true.	(2) We have not been visited by aliens.
Therefore (3) **this** is not true.	Therefore (3) there are no intelligent aliens in our galaxy.

Michael H. Hart, "An Explanation for the Absence of Extraterrestrials on Earth," *Quarterly Journal of the Royal Astronomical Society* 16 (1975): 128–135.

DISJUNCTIVE SYLLOGISM

(1) Either **this** is true or **that** is true.	(1) Either the kidnappers fled into the Fire Swamp or the prince is wrong.
(2) **That** is not true.	(2) The prince is not wrong.
Therefore (3) **this** is true.	Therefore (3) the kidnappers fled into the Fire Swamp.

Rob Reiner, *The Princess Bride* (Century City, CA: 20th Century Fox, 1987).

HYPOTHETICAL SYLLOGISM

(1) If **this** is true, then **that** is true.	(1) If <u>there is no government</u>, then <u>there will be a war of all against all</u>.
(2) If **that** is true, then **that other thing** is true.	(2) If <u>there is a war of all against all</u>, then <u>life will be nasty, brutish, and short</u>.
Therefore (3) if **this** is true, then **that other thing** is true.	Therefore (3) if <u>there is no government</u>, then <u>life will be nasty, brutish, and short</u>.

Thomas Hobbes, *Leviathan* (Indianapolis: Hackett Publishing, 1994 [1651]).

Some patterns closely resemble the deductively valid patterns shown so far but are actually *invalid*. The following examples show two very common invalid patterns; see if you can figure out situations in which the premises of each argument would be true but the conclusions false.

AFFIRMING THE CONSEQUENT

(1) If **this** is true, then **that** is true.	(1) If <u>Fluffy is a dolphin</u>, then <u>Fluffy is a mammal</u>.
(2) **That** is true.	(2) <u>Fluffy is a mammal</u>.
Therefore (3) **this** is true.	Therefore (3) <u>Fluffy is a dolphin</u>.

DENYING THE ANTECEDENT

(1) If **this** is true, then **that** is true.	(1) If <u>Bubbles is a dolphin</u>, then <u>Bubbles is a mammal</u>.
(2) **This** is not true.	(2) <u>Bubbles is not a dolphin</u>.
Therefore (3) **that** is not true.	Therefore (3) <u>Bubbles is not a mammal</u>.

Some deductive arguments are about the connections between kinds or categories of things. Logicians call these arguments **categorical arguments** and the study of them is called **categorical logic**. Here are four of the twenty-four kinds of valid categorical arguments.

CATEGORICAL ARGUMENTS

(1) All <u>X's</u> are <u>Y's</u>.	(1) All <u>liars</u> are <u>bad people</u>.
(2) All <u>Z's</u> are <u>X's</u>.	(2) All <u>politicians</u> are <u>liars</u>.
Therefore (3) all <u>Z's</u> are <u>Y's</u>.	Therefore (3) all <u>politicians</u> are <u>bad people</u>.[1]

(continued on next page)

---

1. Remember that an argument can be valid even if the premises aren't true! Maybe some politicians aren't liars. Maybe some liars aren't bad people. Still, *if* all liars are bad people and all politicians are liars, *then it must be true* that all politicians are bad people.

CATEGORICAL ARGUMENTS (CONT.)

(1) All <u>X's</u> are <u>Y's</u>.	(1) All <u>high school students</u> are <u>people who are under 21</u>.
(2) No <u>Y's</u> are <u>Z's</u>.	(2) No <u>people who are under 21</u> are <u>people who are allowed to drink</u>.
Therefore (3) no <u>Z's</u> are <u>X's</u>.	Therefore (3) no <u>people who are allowed to drink</u> are <u>high school students</u>.

(1) All <u>X's</u> are <u>Y's</u>.	(1) All <u>mammals</u> are <u>animals that nurse their young</u>.
(2) Some <u>X's</u> are <u>Z's</u>.	(2) Some <u>mammals</u> are <u>animals that lay eggs</u>.
Therefore (3) some <u>Z's</u> are <u>Y's</u>.	Therefore (3) some <u>animals that lay eggs</u> are <u>animals that nurse their young</u>.

(continued on next page)

CATEGORICAL ARGUMENTS (CONT.)

(1) Some <u>X's</u> are not <u>Y's</u>.	(1) Some <u>people who auditioned for American Idol</u> are not <u>good singers</u>.
(2) All <u>X's</u> are <u>Z's</u>.	(2) All <u>people who auditioned for American Idol</u> are <u>people who think they can sing</u>.
Therefore (3) some <u>Z's</u> are not <u>Y's</u>.	Therefore (3) some <u>people who think they can sing</u> are not <u>good singers</u>.

Many kinds of categorical arguments are invalid, as illustrated by the following example. Both of the premises in the following example are true, but the conclusion is false.

(1) All <u>X's</u> are <u>Y's</u>.	(1) All <u>dolphins</u> are <u>mammals</u>.
(2) Some <u>Y's</u> are <u>Z's</u>.	(2) Some <u>mammals</u> are <u>creatures that can build rockets</u>.
Therefore (3) some <u>X's</u> are <u>Z's</u>.	Therefore (3) some <u>dolphins</u> are <u>creatures that can build rockets</u>.

Logicians sometimes contrast deductive arguments with inductive arguments, which don't aim to establish their conclusions with certainty. Consider, for instance, the following argument: No one you know has ever shown up to class wearing a chicken costume or had a teacher who showed up to class wearing a chicken costume. Therefore, your teacher will not show up to your next class wearing a chicken costume. Assuming that the first premise is true, this is a reasonably strong argument; it gives you a good reason to believe that your teacher will not show up to your next class wearing a chicken costume. But it doesn't *guarantee* that he or she won't do so; even though the premises are true, it's still *possible* that your teacher will show up to your next class dressed as a giant chicken.

Appendix B

Selected Fallacies

AD HOMINEM (AGAINST THE PERSON)

Criticizing the person who makes a claim or argument rather than criticizing the claim or argument itself.

PERSON 1: The federal government shouldn't raise the minimum wage because that would lead to a lot of poor people losing their jobs.

PERSON 2: You don't really care about poor people! You're just a selfish, rich jerk who is worried that goods and services will become more expensive for you personally if the minimum wage goes up.

ANECDOTAL FALLACY

Using personal anecdotes or vivid examples, rather than adequate data, to support a broad generalization.

My great-grandmother smoked four packs a day for seventy years, and she never got lung cancer. Therefore, cigarettes don't really cause lung cancer.

APPEAL TO AUTHORITY

Illegitimately arguing that a statement is true because an authority figure said so, especially when the statement is outside the authority figure's area of expertise.

Philosophy is useless. The astrophysicist Neil DeGrasse Tyson said so.

APPEAL TO IGNORANCE (*AD IGNORATIUM*)

Arguing that something is true because it can't be proven false.

PERSON 1: Airplanes are secretly spraying chemicals to control our minds!

PERSON 2: That's a nonsense conspiracy theory.

PERSON 1: Can you prove that it's not happening?

APPEAL TO NATURE

Arguing that something is good because it's natural or that it's bad because it's unnatural or artificial.

It's much better to treat illness using natural herbs than with pharmaceuticals. Pharmaceuticals are full of artificial chemicals!

APPEAL TO POPULARITY (*AD POPULUM*)

Arguing that something is true because everyone believes it or that something is good because everyone likes it.

Most Americans agree that the death penalty deters crime. Therefore, the death penalty does deter crime.

CIRCULAR REASONING (BEGGING THE QUESTION)

Including or assuming your conclusion as one of your premises—often as a hidden premise.

PERSON 1: This salesman is trustworthy; he's not going to try to sell me something I don't need just to get the commission.

PERSON 2: How do you know?

PERSON 1: He told me that all he wants is to help me find the best deal.

COMPOSITION

Illegitimately arguing that because something is true of each part of something, it's also true of the whole; or that because something is true of each member of a group, it's true of the group as a whole.

My greenhouse gas emissions don't make any difference to the climate. Nor does my neighbor's, or my friend's, or any other individual's emissions. Therefore, humanity's greenhouse gas emissions don't make any difference to the climate.

DIVISION

Illegitimately arguing that because something is true of a group or thing as a whole, it's also true of each part.

The United States is rich. Therefore, all Americans are rich.

EQUIVOCATION

Using the same word or phrase in two different ways to make it seem like an argument works when it really doesn't.

This school is a drug-free zone. Caffeine is a drug, and coffee has caffeine in it. Therefore, coffee isn't allowed in this school.

FALSE DICHOTOMY (FALSE DILEMMA)

Falsely assuming that there are only two options in order to argue *for* one of them simply by arguing *against* the other.

The Egyptians built the Great Pyramid to align with magnetic north. Since they didn't have compasses, that's either a complete coincidence or aliens helped them build it. There's no way the Great Pyramid's alignment is just a coincidence. Thus, aliens helped the Egyptians build the Great Pyramid.

GENETIC FALLACY

Arguing that a statement is false or an argument is weak because of the source (i.e., the genesis) of that statement or argument.

PERSON 1: Your uncle told me that I should start saving for retirement in my twenties because then my retirement investments will have much more time to grow, and I'll end up with a lot more money when I retire.

PERSON 2: What!? Don't listen to my uncle! He gives terrible advice!

HASTY GENERALIZATION

Arguing for a sweeping generalization on the basis of too few examples or examples that aren't representative of the group as a whole.

Only one of my friends was enthusiastic about Hillary Clinton for president. Therefore, very few Americans were enthusiastic about Hillary Clinton for president.

POST HOC FALLACY (POST HOC, ERGO PROPTER HOC)

Illegitimately arguing that because one event happened after another event, the earlier event caused the later event. From a Latin phrase meaning "after this, therefore because of this."

I got a flu shot, and the next day I came down with the flu. The flu shot must have given me the flu.

SLIPPERY SLOPE

Arguing that something shouldn't be done because it would inevitably lead to some unacceptable outcome, without giving adequate reasons to think that the first thing really would lead to an unacceptable outcome.

It's not that there's anything wrong with adults using marijuana recreationally. But if we legalize marijuana, then before long, we'll have middle schoolers snorting cocaine and shooting heroin.

STRAWMAN

Arguing against a distorted, weaker version of someone's statement or argument rather than against the real statement or argument.

PERSON 1: This country should implement stricter gun control laws because they'd reduce the number of gun deaths.

PERSON 2: Nonsense! Universal background checks wouldn't eliminate gun deaths, so there's no point in imposing them on law-abiding citizens.